Are We Growing?

Some Personal Experiences in Seeking Happiness

Loran Joly

ReEnvision Press

Contents

Chapter One

For Those who Seek...

This book is particularly for:

The Seekers.

The Curious.

The Ponderers.

Those who wonder why this doesn't jive with that...

Those who seek to understand.

And to those who desire

to hear what others have to say...

Valade
en Corrèze
DE FRUITS
DEPUIS 1932
Jus d'Orange
BOPI
Teneur en fruits 100%

Let us scoop up Wisdom

This book is also dedicated to everyone
who does not believe that everything has already
been figured out already...

"Of making books thereof making many books there is no end." Solomon, King of Israel and Judah. Ecclesiastes 12:12

So,

might our best credentials

be the proofs of our curiosity,

our Seeking,

and our Notebooks, even,

the cookbooks we

wrote ourselves?

Ingredients
- garlic
- fish sauce!
- Chilli
- ground pork
- basil
- Oyster Sauce
- Sugar
- Carrot (just kidding)
no we don't use carrot!

For,

We have plenty of Learners,

plenty of Downloaders.

But how many are seeking to Figure Out what needs figuring out, instead of Learning what supposedly has already been figured out?

We hear,

"Don't reinvent the wheel".

But, please show me who did a very good job inventing wheels, when it comes to something as complex as the human being?

***

Wheels, that's easy.

People? Well, that's Rocket Science!

So, might we

Get Cracking, before our world – and ourselves, of course,

Get Cracked?

We Snooze, We Lose?

Chapter Two

Know Thyself - Better and Better?

Who are we? Or perhaps the more important question is, "Who do some others desire us to think we are not?" "And why?"

We might also consider:

"All of humanity's problems stem from man's inability to sit quietly in a room alone." —— Blaise Pascal, Pensées

We are all on a search to be the happiest we can, surely.
This likely includes seeking clarity on "Who we are",
or as Socrates urged,
"Know Thyself".

We might also say, that to Know Ourself also includes,

to Know Others, too; and how we are both similar and different.

As such, this short book is a brief spin on this route of clarifying identity, to increase happiness.

It is also a sharing with others, of a part of a journey of this author.

Chapter Three

The Role of Curiosity: Hard to Define, but Surely CRUCIAL!

1. Einstein was said to be CURIOUS, and that it was THIS CURIOSITY which SET him APART:

Curious?

See VIDEO:

"Albert Einstein and the Power of Curiosity"

"Discover the fascinating life of Albert Einstein, a genius driven by curiosity! In this video, we delve into Einstein's unconventional childhood, his delayed speech and school struggles, and how a small compass ignited his quest to uncover the universe's mysteries. Learn about Einstein's clashes with teachers, his groundbreaking theories, and the revolutionary equation $E=mc^2$. Explore how

his imaginative thought experiments and relentless curiosity laid the foundation for advancements in quantum mechanics and GPS technology. Join us in celebrating the enduring impact of Einstein's curiosity-driven approach on science and innovation."

https://youtu.be/e-DlCY28fT0

2. The IDEAS of RICHARD FEYNMAN (physicist, Nobel-Prize winner):

When I lived in a hovel in California, around 1988, I had purchased Richard Feynman's book,
"Surely You're Joking, Mr. Feynman!".
I was bowled over.

***

In particular, might we consider this comment, by Feynman, in the final chapter of this book?

> The final chapter, "Cargo Cult Science," was adapted from Feynman's 1974 commencement address at the California Institute of Technology, in which he cautioned graduates not to minimize the weaknesses of their research in the pursuit of a preferred conclusion.
>
> ...
>
> He drew an analogy to the cargo cult phenomenon in the South Pacific Ocean in which, as he understood it, islanders built a mock airstrip to cause airplanes loaded with imported goods to land. Similarly, he argued, adopting the appearances of scientific investigation without a self-critical attitude will fail to produce reliable results.

Feynman's "cargo cult" metaphor was used by Tomasz Witkowski in his criticism of social science and psychology in particular. In the first part of his book, Psychology Led Astray, Witkowski asks "Is Psychology a Cargo Cult Science?", pointing out that the growth in the number of psychologists world wide has been parallel with a decrease in mental health. He also points to other articles applying the cargo cult metaphor to criticize social sciences."

https://en.wikipedia.org/wiki/Surely_You%27re_Joking,_Mr._Feynman!

Secondly, there are fascinating videos about the curiosity of Feynman, too, such as:

"What Makes Everything Work | Richard Feynman | Curiosity":

https://youtu.be/JbesmfdUMkw

3. My experiences in having met LOGGERS, in Appalachia:

One cited how he LEARNED MORE, about PEOPLE, by CURIOUSLY OBSERVING ANIMALS, than from ANY OTHER source of information:

Another observer of life...

Chapter Four

On Thinking, vs "FACTOID"- Collecting

1. FIRST,

the VIEW of EINSTEIN:

From a video entitled "Was Albert Einstein a fraud genius?":

A video CLAIMS:

"Did you know, Albert Einstein, ... , DID NOT MEMORIZE ANYTHING?

...

" I do not CARRY such information IN my HEAD, since it is READILY AVAILABLE in BOOK.

The Ability to THINK is MUCH GREATER than the ABILITY to MEMORIZE FACTS"

(From YouTube video):

"Einstein's Surprising Response"

https://www.youtube.com/shorts/W4rlCWgG8LQ?feature=share

***

The AUTHOR of THIS book, however, would ADD, as a *COROLLARY*:

That EINSTEIN and many other Mind – Greats,

DO, in fact, MEMORIZE;

Memorizing of what WE see as FACTS, IS surely a CRUCIAL concept.

ONLY,

these are not FACTS that they memorize,

i.e. FACTOIDS, which ARE in PRINT;

But RATHER,

they MEMORIZE, The SECRET SAUCE PRINCIPLES,

Which one CANNOT look up in "REFERENCE MANUALS" (e.g. PRINTED books).

And,

THESE "ITEMS"

are ONLY discovered

FOR *OURSELVES*,

and then *DO* Require MEMORIZING,

And the FIRST STEP is in

NOTETAKING:

"What are your credentials?" Our credentials are OUR TOOLS, including our NOTES! Talk softly and CARRY a BIG SET of NOTE-BOOKS!

PRECISELY because THESE facts

are NOT to be found IN books?

THESE facts are perhaps the
SECRET SAUCE facts,
the RECIPE – FACTS that
are HIDDEN facts.
The SECRET is in the SPICES!

Chapter Five

Are We Growing or Are We Stalled?

Freud referred to certain people as having "fixations".

In terms of being fixated to one or more defense mechanisms, likely.

Perhaps, fixated in our denials, a set of such defenses.

Might we say, in general, that to be fixated, in a number of areas, is to be "Stalled Out"?

Or, as Florence Scovel Shinn called it, to have "logjams"?

Others refer to having "Limiting Beliefs".

While Gloria Steinem talks of the need to Unlearn....

***

So, perhaps our ideas can use a bit of scrubbing – or a lot of scrubbing?

So that our lives can "flow" better?

I was once told, by a boss, "Don't Go There!" Don't look too closely ... Aka If we ask questions, our lives will change!

Chapter Six

Some People Say That We Need to Unlearn This and That...

"The first problem for all of us, men and women, is not to learn, but to unlearn."
(Gloria Steinem.)

https://elevatesociety.com/the-first-problem-for-all/

***

Also see:

https://www.brainyquote.com/photos_tr/en/g/gloriasteinem/164928/gloriasteinem1-2x.jpg

From:

"Gloria Steinem Quotes." BrainyQuote.com. BrainyMedia Inc, 2024. 25 December 2024.

https://www.brainyquote.com/quotes/gloria_steinem_164928

OTHER quotes by Gloria Steinem:

https://www.brainyquote.com/lists/authors/top-10-gloria-steinem-quotes

Chapter Seven

Viewing Life From a Bird's Eye View?

This book is an idea sketch, not a definitive study.

So, it has inaccuracies.

And it has "typos", in general.

However, if there is one thing I had to say I most learned from Ajahn Brahm, a Buddhist monk, after watching over twenty of his videos, it is this:

That there is no such thing as imperfection.

I do add, that I am not a Buddhist, per say.

In fact, I do not try to classify myself in a box.

One might say I am of the Religion of the Mutt, or adhere to the Philosophy of the Mutt, or the Weltanschauung of the Smorgasbord:

The so-called Mutt is a collection - an amalgam - or Smorgasbord - of genes - or IDEAS. The Mutt thus is not bred to have only one central idea. The Mutt is an Eclectic, a Renaissance Item, an Autodidact, a Trail-Blazer? A Creature which "Follows the Beat of its Own Drum"?

This is my view on the options in life, to be consu med...

We are surely quite limited in view, if this is our food for thought, day in, day out?

So,

This author specializes partly in seeking a bird's-eye view of life.

As has Tenzin Palmo, one might say.

"She is an author, teacher and founder of the Dongyu Gatsal Ling Nunnery in Himachal Pradesh, India. She is best known for being one of the very few Western yoginis trained in the

East, having spent twelve years living in a remote cave in the Himalayas, three of those years in strict meditation retreat."

https://en.wikipedia.org/wiki/Tenzin_Palmo

For more, see:

"Cave in the Snow Documentary - The Story of Jetsunma Tenzin Palmo":

https://youtu.be/XyP1PezzVdY

As such, I am not oriented, any more, toward polishing dust and smudges in my writings.

To myself, the idea is far more important than the shell it comes in.

We need the overall picture...

Chapter Eight

Getting Lost in a Sea of Data?

"I went to the woods because I wished to live deliberately, to front only the essential facts of life, and see if I could not learn what it had to teach, and not, when I came to die, discover that I had not lived. I did not wish to live what was not life, living is so dear; nor did I wish to practise resignation, unless it was quite necessary. I wanted to live deep and suck out all the marrow of life, to live so sturdily and Spartan-like as to put to rout all that was not life, to cut a broad swath and shave close, to drive life into a corner, and reduce it to its lowest terms..." (Henry David Thoreau).

(This cabin is not Thoreau's, but along the same idea...)

Chapter Nine

Catalysts?

With deep regard for Mr. Shinichi Suzuki:

Please see

"Nurtured by Love DVD Preview":

https://youtu.be/ZBjKw7KOwd8

and

https://internationalsuzuki.org/shinichisuzuki.htm

"Book Review: Nurtured by Love"

Audrey Rindlisbacher:

https://youtu.be/mWDVCuYJh_Y

Also:

"Suzuki Book Club discussing Nurtured by Love, Dr. Suzuki, on 24th May 2020 with Kate Conway."

https://youtu.be/FUwaFCtVlyo

Shinichi Suzuki may have influenced this writer more than he can presently fathom,

inasmuch as this writer studied Suzuki violin, first from a graduate student

at the University of North Carolina, Chapel Hill,

then at the MacPhail Center for Music,

under the guidance of Mark Bjork,

who in turn had studied

under the famous violinist

Josef Gingold

See "Josef Gingold profile (1984)":

https://youtu.be/Rn3-fF1tYo0

And,

"Gingold The Love of Music":

https://youtu.be/7AxANytDBJI

"Bjork has some fascinating perspectives and ideas about teaching, having personally studied with both Josef Gingold, at Indiana University, and with Shinichi Suzuki, whose teaching he observed on a daily basis for four months in Matumoto in the early '70s."

https://www.violinist.com/blog/laurie/20173/21035/

***

"Mark is recognized internationally as a leader in the field of Suzuki Talent Education. In 1967 he started one of the first Suzuki programs in the United States at the MacPhail Center for the Arts, which was part of the University of Minnesota at the time. Workshops, master classes and clinics, often related to Suzuki Talent Education, have taken him throughout the U.S., Canada, South America, Europe, Australia, New Zealand, Korea, and Japan. His former students include concertmasters, chamber music performers, and teachers. Mark is the author of "Expanding Horizons: the Suzuki Trained Violinist Grows Up."

https://mplspops.org/player-profile-mark-bjork/

***

Also see? ...

https://www.macphail.org/faculty/mark-bjork/

BELOW:

This author, playing in one of the Suzuki group performances managed by Mark Bjork, in Minneapolis, Minnesota

Author, back row, in a Suzuki performance under the guidance of Mark Bjork.

This author was slated to go on a tour throughout Russia, with his orchestra, immediately after graduating from High School, but canceled out at the last minute, largely because his father believed his son would be destined for abject financial poverty if he continued with the violin...

Chapter Ten

School Ourselves or BE Schooled"?

A photograph - or image - is Worth a Thousand Words?

A photograph is worth a thousand words?

See "The Power of Photography: How Photographs Changed Our Lives", by Vickie Goldberg.

Note: This author started in with photography when he was seven, by sending bubble gum wrappers to a company, in exchange for a black-and-white box camera. His father also had an influence, in this regard. Then, in his twenties, he would hang out, on the weekends, at Balboa Park, in San Diego, California, at its Museum of Photographic Arts, with his Leica camera – to impress the gals? - and also take part in field trips with the camera club, there – also located at Balboa Park.

In his thirties, he studied with the New York Institute of Photography, to garner some further insights.

He now has three fully operational photography websites.

But this, only after having polished away his perfectionism, which essentially involved collecting every conceivable photography book, gadget, and other "tool of the trade", and substituting it all with JUST DOING IT, as per the phrase, "80% EQUALS DONE".

Be willing to look flawed?

We often start out joyous

We start out SEEKERS!

But then,

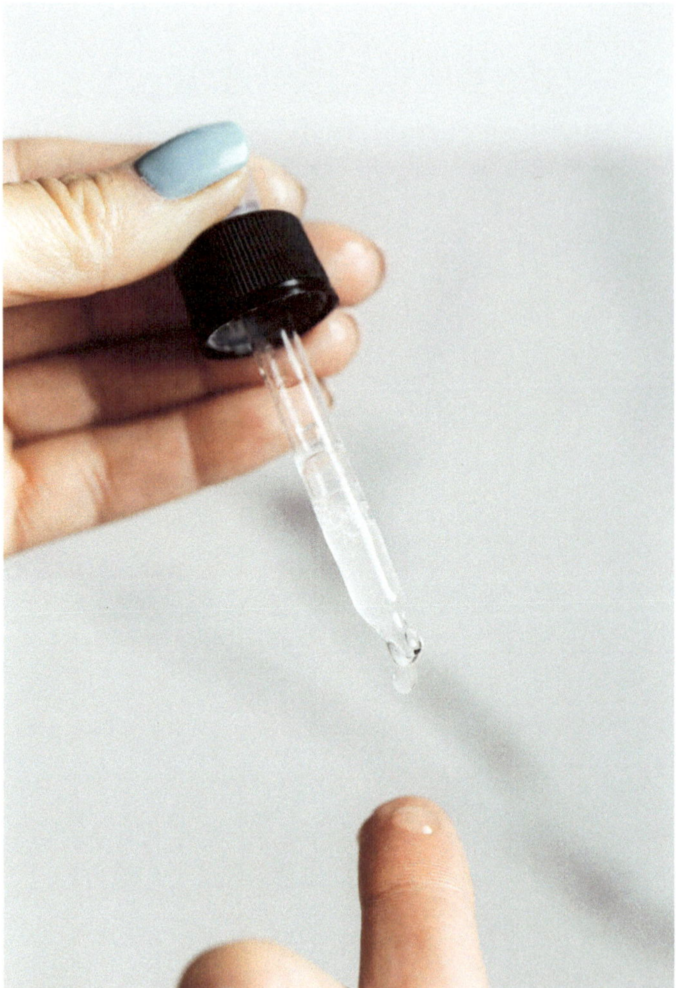

Our world seems to titrate Happiness to us!

We conform? To being so similar to others, that we cannot be criticized, and have to define, for ourselves, who we are?

"Society is characterized by 'the smooth mediocrity and squalid contentment of the times' and it is the job of the individual to 'hurl in the face of custom, and trade, and office, the fact which is the upshot of all history, that there is a great responsible Thinker and Actor working wherever a man works.'"

https://www.litcharts.com/lit/self-reliance/themes/non-conformity-morality-and-individual-greatness

POND'S
Rexona
Curl Talk
ULTIMATE

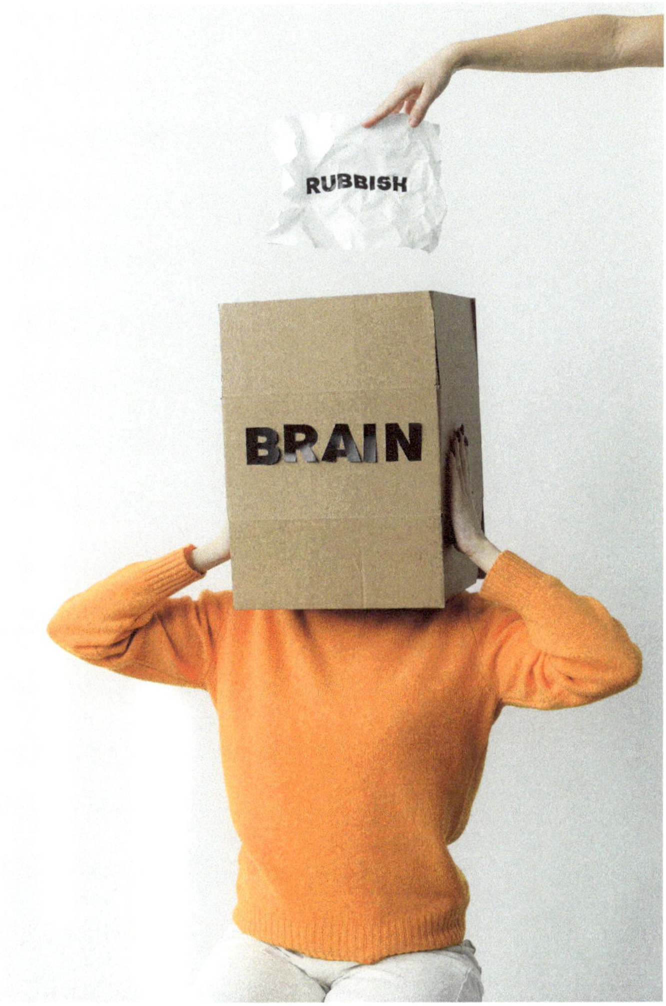

"Get" a "Good Education", or "Self-Educate"?

Thank goodness we have evolved so far...

"One man's meat is another man's poison." Pascal Tréguer

"From Whom All Blessings Flow"?

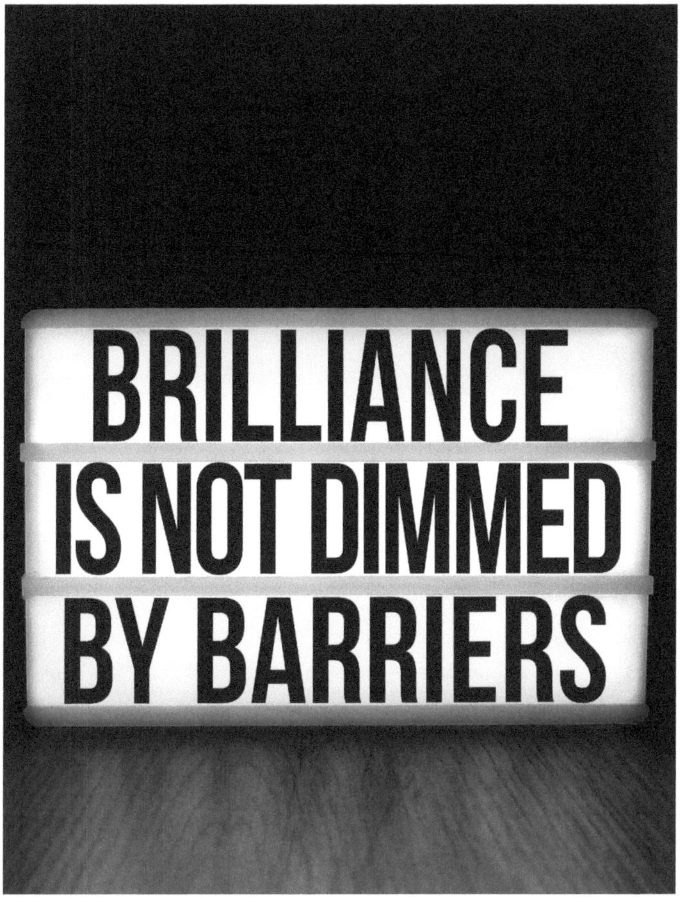
BRILLIANCE
IS NOT DIMMED
BY BARRIERS

Today's scientific, thoroughly tested facts, might just be tomorrow's ...?

How much of useful therapy is simply - or not so simply - the validating of what mom and pop and grandma told us, before Some Others came along and added their two cents' worth?

Regarding Some People's Two Cents' Worth, might we ponder

"The Emperor's New Clothes", a story by Hans Christian Anderson:

"The weavers report that the emperor's suit is finished. They mime dressing him and he sets off in a procession before the whole city. The townsfolk uncomfortably go along with the pretense, not wanting to appear inept or stupid, until a child blurts out that the emperor is wearing nothing at all. The people then realize that everyone has been fooled. Although startled, the emperor continues the procession, walking more proudly than ever. The fate of the con-men is not revealed."

https://en.wikipedia.org/wiki/The_Emperor%27s_New_Clothes#Commentaries

If we believe what some desire us to believe, they may be happier, at least for a time; but what about ourselves?

Alternatively, ...

Chapter Eleven

Comments About the Terms "Writers" and "Books"

Naturally, this book is not fully polished.

Perhaps this is not even a book, thus?

A book is a Polished Package of Sheets of Idealized Paper, a coffee table Ornament:

How many books are for display?

Is a book a decorative item?

A "BOOK" Might Be a Collection of Words, produced by Writers? Whereas a Collection of Wisdom has no Label, and is produced by Artists?

Also, might we ponder the words I heard, a year ago, from someone in a village in Appalachia:

"I used to read a lot, but can no longer find anything worth reading..."

Tower of Babel, or Tower of Words?

Words never cease.

Or,

Is a Quasi-Book a Font of Truer Knowledge?

Gore Vidal once said, "In every generation, there are a few unfortunate souls who are condemned, practically at birth, to be that absolute absurdity;

a writer for life." Yet, be it known, that Vidal was also an enigma to many.

"I don't care to belong to a club that accepts people like me as members." Groucho Marx. Image by author of this book.

Chapter Twelve

If We Don't Grow, We Are Left Behind?

ВОДА

PLEASE DESTROY CELL
PHONES BEFORE ENTERING

Chapter Thirteen

A Few Family Photos Which Tell a Story

The author's influences include a couple of images from the family, who are or were war refugees from the very eastern reaches of Eastern Europe:

From the village of Piaski, Poland, a mere nine miles from Ukraine, and a major point for the incursion of the Soviets, in 1939, when the author's mother was not quite two years of age.

Photograph of my mother, left, at the age of two; my grandmother, center, and a helper, right, 1940, as war refugees in Poland, during World War II

And, summers at his Eastern European relatives' farm in Michigan, during childhood years...

Author's great-grandmother, in back-ground; mother, right, and myself, left at the age of about seven

The author's grandparents, with whom he spent his summers, as a youth, on their farm. His grandfather, right, also played the violin.

The author's mother, in Europe, before emigrating to America, first by way of Ellis Island.

The author's mother, when she was about twenty-five:

Author, left; mother, middle; sister, right

A map of Poland:

Poland, including a view of Lubelskie, right-most, where the author's mother was born. Her father was born in Ukraine, and spoke Ukrainian, and was a Mennonite. He and the author built woodworking projects, together, on his farm. iStock Photos

Chapter Fourteen

The Author

The author welcomes your comments and your own personal experiences in general, and can be reached at

message@goldpogo.com

He lives in a village of 15,000.

A vista, one hour from the author's present village.

www.ingramcontent.com/pod-product-compliance
Ingram Content Group UK Ltd.
Pitfield, Milton Keynes, MK11 3LW, UK
UKHW062019030826
14089UKWH00029B/169